A Guide for Using

The Secret Garden

in the Classroom

Based on the novel written by
Frances Hodgson Burnett

*This guide written by **Concetta Doti Ryan***
*and illustrated by **Keith Vasconcelles***

Teacher Created Resources
12621 Western Avenue
Garden Grove, CA 92841
www.teachercreated.com
ISBN: 978-1-55734-414-4
©1992 Teacher Created Resources
Reprinted, 2016
Made in U.S.A.

Table of Contents

Introduction

A good book can touch our lives like a good friend. Within its pages are words and characters that can inspire us to achieve our highest ideals. We can turn to it for companionship, recreation, comfort, and guidance. It also gives us a cherished story to hold in our hearts forever.

In *Literature Units,* great care has been taken to select books that are sure to become good friends!

Teachers who use this literature unit will find the following features to supplement their own valuable ideas.

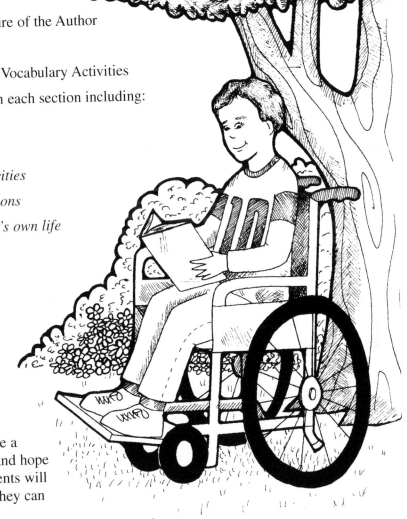

- Sample Lesson Plans
- Pre-reading Activities
- A Biographical Sketch and Picture of the Author
- A Book Summary
- Vocabulary Lists and Suggested Vocabulary Activities
- Chapters grouped for study, with each section including:

    - *quizzes*
    - *hands-on projects*
    - *cooperative learning activities*
    - *cross-curriculum connections*
    - *extensions into the reader's own life*

- Post-reading Activities
- Book Report Ideas
- Research Ideas
- A Culminating Activity
- Three Unit Test Options
- Bibliography
- Answer Key

We are confident that this unit will be a valuable addition to your planning, and hope that, as you use our ideas, your students will increase the circle of "friends" that they can have in books!

Sample Lesson Plan

Each of the lessons suggested below can take from one to several days to complete.

Lesson 1

- Introduce and complete some or all of the pre-reading activities found on page 5.
- Read "About the Author" with your students. (page 6)
- Introduce vocabulary for Section 1. (page 8)
- Have students suggest definitions.

Lesson 2

- Read chapters 1-7. Place vocabulary in context and discuss meanings.
- Play a vocabulary game. (page 9)
- Draw the garden. (page 11)
- Write nursery rhymes. (page 12)
- Discuss the book in terms of science. (page 13)
- Begin "Reading Response Journals." (page 15)
- Administer the Section 1 quiz. (page 10)
- Introduce vocabulary for Section 2. (page 8)
- Have students suggest definitions.

Lesson 3

- Read chapters 8-11. Place vocabulary in context and discuss meanings.
- Play a vocabulary game. (page 9)
- Research types of flowers. (page 17)
- Complete personality profiles. (page 18)
- Research robins. (page 19)
- Compare home life. (page 20)
- Administer the Section 2 quiz. (page 16)
- Introduce vocabulary for Section 3. (page 8)
- Have students suggest definitions.

Lesson 4

- Read chapters 12-18. Place vocabulary in context and discuss meanings.
- Play a vocabulary game. (page 9)
- Write a thank you letter. (page 22)
- Find out about a new language. (page 23)
- Discuss the book in terms of physical education. (page 24)

- Have some rainy day fun! (page 25)
- Administer the Section 3 quiz. (page 21)
- Introduce vocabulary for Section 4. (page 8)
- Have students suggest definitions.

Lesson 5

- Read chapters 19-23. Place vocabulary in context and discuss meanings.
- Play a vocabulary game. (page 9)
- Write an advice column. (page 27)
- Visit a nursery. (page 28)
- Discuss the book in terms of cooking. (page 29)
- Get to know a character. (page 30)
- Administer the Section 4 quiz. (page 26)
- Introduce vocabulary for Section 5. (page 8)
- Have students suggest definitions.

Lesson 6

- Read chapters 24- 28. Place vocabulary in context and discuss meanings.
- Play a vocabulary game. (page 9)
- Draw a new secret garden. (page 32)
- Look to the future. (page 33)
- Complete a crossword puzzle. (page 34)
- Design your own secret place. (page 35)
- Administer the Section 5 quiz. (page 31)

Lesson 7

- Discuss any questions your students may have about the story. (page 36)
- Assign book reports and research projects. (pages 37 and 38)
- Begin work on culminating activity. (pages 39, 40, and 41)

Lesson 8

- Administer Unit Tests: 1, 2, and/or 3. (pages 42, 43, and 44)
- Discuss test possibilities and answers.
- Discuss students' enjoyment of the book.
- Provide a list of related reading. (page 45)

Before the Book

Before you begin reading *The Secret Garden* with your students, do some pre-reading activities to stimulate interest and enhance comprehension. Here are some activities that might work well in your class.

1. Predict what the story might be about just by hearing the title.

2. Predict what the story might be about just by looking at the cover illustration.

3. Discuss other books by Frances Hodgson Burnett that students may have read or heard about. For example: *Sara Crewe; A Little Princess; Little Lord Fauntleroy.*

4. Answer these questions:

   • Are you interested in:

     – stories about children who become very close friends?
     – stories about reaching difficult goals?
     – stories about secrets?
     – stories that involve animals?
     – stories about plants and gardens?
     – stories about mysterious houses?

   • Would you ever:

     – try to find something that you weren't supposed to find?
     – become good friends with a member of the opposite sex?
     – work very hard on something you are committed to?
     – be able to keep a special secret?

   • Have you ever planted anything before?

5. Work in groups or as a class to write a story that involves an animal helping the characters reach a goal.

About the Author

Frances Hodgson Burnett was born on November 24, 1849, in Manchester, England. Her father, Edwin, was a hardware dealer. He died when Frances was just four years old. Frances' mother, Eliza, was left to take care of the family. The family struggled to make ends meet. Finally, when Frances was 15, she and her family moved to Tennessee.

In 1867 Frances decided to submit a manuscript to a publisher. Her first story, *Miss Desborough's Difficulties* sold for twenty dollars. By Frances' eighteenth birthday she was a published writer. In October, 1886 the classic *Little Lord Fauntleroy* was published. This story is about a model little gentleman in very proper costume and curls. It immediately became one of the biggest sellers of all time. In 1888 the story opened on Broadway as a full length play. Also in 1888, Frances' popular story about a girl named Sara Crewe was published. Sara Crewe attends a boarding school. While she is there, her father's reversal of fortune causes her to become a charity student. Although her status in the school is changed she behaves as a princess. Later, this story was expanded and renamed *A Little Princess.*

It wasn't until 1911 that *The Secret Garden* was published. Frances wrote about gardens in her childhood years. They had long since been an interest of hers. She writes, "I love to kneel down on the grass at the edge of a flower bed and pull out weeds fiercely and throw them into a heap by my side. I love to fight with those who can spring up again almost in a night and taunt me. I tear them up by the roots again and again, and when at last after many days, perhaps, it seems as if I had beaten them for a time at least, I go away feeling like an army with banners."

The Secret Garden has proven itself to be a timeless novel. Today, more than 80 years after its publication, the story is still popular. Several years ago the book was adapted into a Hallmark Hall of Fame special on television. It has been made into a Broadway musical in 1991 and is often performed.

(The information and quotation for this biographical sketch were taken from *Yesterday's Authors of Books for Children,* Volume 2, pages 32-49)

The Secret Garden

by Frances Hodgson Burnett

The Phillips Publishing Company, 1911; Dell, 1984

Available in Canada from Doubleday Publishing and in U.K from Penguin

Mary Lennox is a disagreeable young girl living in India. An outbreak of cholera which claims the lives of many people, including Mary's parents, leaves Mary an orphan. She is sent to live in Yorkshire, England with her only relative, Archibald Craven.

Mary has a difficult time adjusting to her new home because in India she was accustomed to having servants wait on her hand and foot. To Mary's surprise, Martha, the maid assigned to caring for Mary, does not respond to her demands. Mrs. Medlock, the woman in charge, takes no interest in her. If this isn't enough, Mr. Craven does not care to see her when she arrives at his house, Misselthwaite Manor.

Mary is quite bored at Misselthwaite Manor because she can find nothing to do. Martha suggests she play out on the moors. She tells Mary the fresh air might do her some good. Mary agrees and while out playing on the moors she meets a gardener, Ben Weatherstaff, and a beautiful robin. Mary is intrigued by the story Ben tells her about the secret garden that has been locked up for ten years. Mr. Craven locked it and threw away the key when his wife fell from a branch to her death. Mary becomes determined to find the key and unlock the secret garden. With the help of the magical robin, she accomplishes her goal.

The garden is terribly overgrown and requires immediate attention if it is ever to become beautiful again. Mary solicits the help of Martha's brother Dickon, a boy who has a special gift for communicating with nature. Together Mary and Dickon begin clearing and planting in the garden. Unfortunately, shortly after they begin, a week of rain restricts them from visiting the garden. During this period of extreme boredom, Mary decides to explore the mansion. To her surprise, she finds a young boy her own age.

Colin is Mr. Craven's son. He stays in bed all day because he fears that he is going to die. He is sure that he will have a hunchback like his father. Mary convinces him that he is fine and eventually talks him into helping her and Dickon to plant the secret garden.

Martha's mother, Mrs. Sowerby writes to Mr. Craven, who is on vacation, and tells him that he should come home. Mrs. Sowerby is one of the only people that knows what the children are doing in the garden. When Mr. Craven returns he is overwhelmed by what the children have done. However, his greatest joy is seeing his son running and playing in the garden.

Vocabulary Lists

On this page are vocabulary lists which correspond to each sectional grouping of chapters. Vocabulary activity ideas can be found on page 9 of this book.

SECTION 1

cross	queer
hunchback	moor
contrary	vexed
corridor	bungalow
conceited	cholera
desolation	disagreeable
dreary	imperious
disdain	governess
massive	languid

SECTION 2

crocus	awkward
inquire	trowel
scullery	determined
vain	impudence
tendrils	reluctant
spade	astonished
intimate	rheumatics

SECTION 3

exultant	guardian
miserable	brocade
mournful	hysterics
invalid *(noun)*	obliged
obstinately	torrents
tremulously	wretched
rebellious	
tantrum	
brooch	

SECTION 4

bewitched	condescended
waft	wick
menagerie	morbid
cautious	shrewd
unscrupulous	elaborate
recluse	canopy
devote	endure
dignity	
perplexed	

SECTION 5

revelation	mystified
desperation	hypochondriac
bounteous	gibberish
devour	currants
inspiration	peculiar
intruder	intervals
vigor	adoration

8

Vocabulary Activity Ideas

You can help your students learn and retain the vocabulary in *The Secret Garden* by providing them with interesting vocabulary activities. Here are a few ideas to try.

❑ Challenge your students to a **Vocabulary Bee!** This is similar to a spelling bee, but in addition to spelling each word correctly, the game participants must correctly define the words as well.

❑ As a group activity, have students work together to create an **Illustrated Dictionary** of the vocabulary words.

❑ Play **20 Clues** with the entire class. In this game, one student selects a vocabulary word and gives clues about this word, one by one, until someone in the class can guess the word.

❑ Play **Vocabulary Charades.** In this game, vocabulary words are acted out.

❑ Encourage students to keep a **Vocabulary Journal** where they can list words they are unfamiliar with, but did not appear on the vocabulary list.

❑ Have students locate the vocabulary word in the story. Proceed to have them guess the meaning by using **Context Clues.**

❑ Challenge students to find **Synonyms or Antonyms** for the vocabulary words from within the story.

❑ Play **Vocabulary Concentration.** The goal of this game is to match vocabulary words with their definitions. Divide the class into groups of 2-5 students. Have the students make two sets of cards the same size and color. On one set have them write the vocabulary words. On the second set have them write the definitions. All cards are mixed together and placed face down on the table. A player picks two cards. If the pair matches the word with its definition, the player keeps the card and takes another turn. If the cards don't match, they are returned to their places face down on the table, and another player takes a turn. Players must concentrate to remember the locations of the words and their definitions. The game continues until all matches have been made. This is an ideal activity for free exploration time.

❑ Have students complete the **Crossword Puzzle** contained in this unit.

Quiz Time!

1. On the back of this paper, write a one paragraph summary of the major events in each chapter of this section. Then complete the rest of the questions on this page.

2. Why does Mary have to live with her uncle? _____

_____

3. What is Mary's first impression of Misselthwaite Manor?_____

_____

4. What does Martha think of Mary? _____

_____

5. Who is Dickon and what is he like? _____

_____

6. Why did Mr. Craven lock the garden?_____

_____

7. What did Mary do when it rained and she could not play outside? _____

_____

8. What did Mrs. Medlock do when she found Mary wandering around? _____

_____

9. Where does Mary want Martha to take her? _____

_____

10. On the back of this paper, draw either the inside or outside of Misselthwaite Manor.

Picture This!

The secret garden has been locked up for ten years now. No one has been inside to care for the grass, trees, and flowers. What do you suppose the garden looks like after all the years of neglect? Draw a picture of what you think the garden may look like right now. Be sure to keep this picture after you finish. It will be needed for a later assignment.

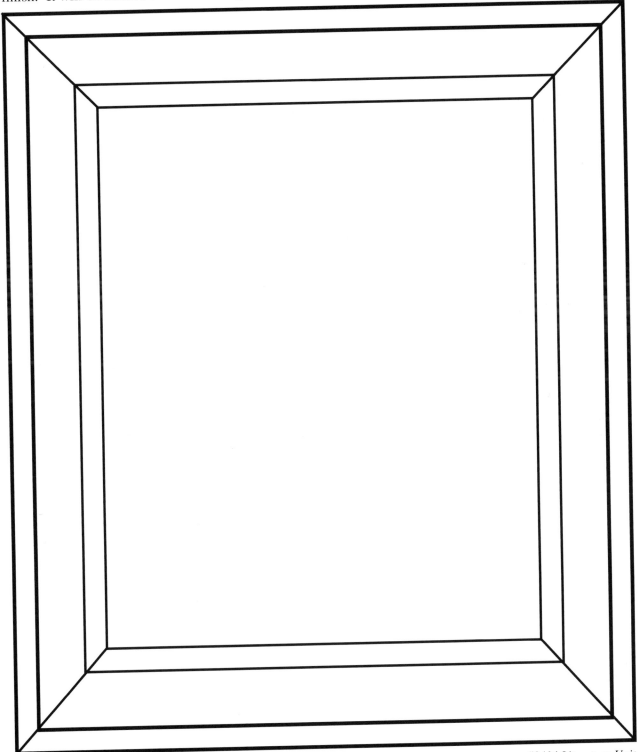

Nursery Rhymes

Mary has a difficult time while staying at the clergyman's house. His children do not like her at all. In fact, they call her "Mistress Mary, quite contrary." This expression came from a nursery rhyme the children sang about Mary.

> *Mistress Mary, quite contrary,*
> *How does your garden grow?*
> *With silver bells, and cockle shells*
> *And marigolds all in a row.*

Conduct some research regarding this nursery rhyme to find out where and when it originated. With a partner, find out if there are more lines than those listed above, or if any lines are different.

What were your favorite nursery rhymes as a child? Recite them to your partner.

With a partner, write an original nursery rhyme. Be sure to include some appropriate illustrations. Write it on separate paper and copy it in the box below. Share it with a kindergarten or first grade class.

(Title)

Your Own Garden

Mary has always been interested in gardening. In India and at the clergyman's house, she plays outside pretending that she has a garden. Now, at Misselthwaite Manor, she is fascinated by all the gardens and enjoys exploring them every day.

Have you ever planted flowers or vegetables? If you have, then you know the excitement of observing the growth of what you've planted. If you have never planted seeds, this activity will be an excellent introduction into the world of plant growth.

Before you begin planting seeds, you should take the time to learn more about them. For example, you can learn what the inside of a seed looks like by dissecting a lima bean.

Try It: Soak lima beans in water overnight. Carefully remove the outer covering of the bean. What is inside the bean? Make a small sketch below.

It is now time to plant your own seeds. Large packets of seeds can be obtained from local gardening stores. Your seeds can be planted in milk cartons. The cartons can be almost any size: quart, pint, or even the small cartons many students receive in their lunches. The last item needed is soil. Again, this can be obtained inexpensively from gardening stores.

Try it: Place soil in carton, filling it to the half way point. Place several seeds in the soil. Cover with a little more soil and add a few drops of water.

Answer the questions below.

- What did you plant?

- How much sunlight does your plant require?

- How often will you need to water your plant?

- Chart your plant's growth over the next few weeks using the chart on page 14. Measure the plant with a ruler and fill in the length on the bar graph, or hold the plant against the graph and mark its length, filling in the bar.

Teacher's note: Lima beans that have been soaked in water can be used for planting.

Charting Plant Growth

Using the graph below, chart the growth of the seeds you planted on page 13.

Date seeds planted: _____

Types of seeds planted: _____

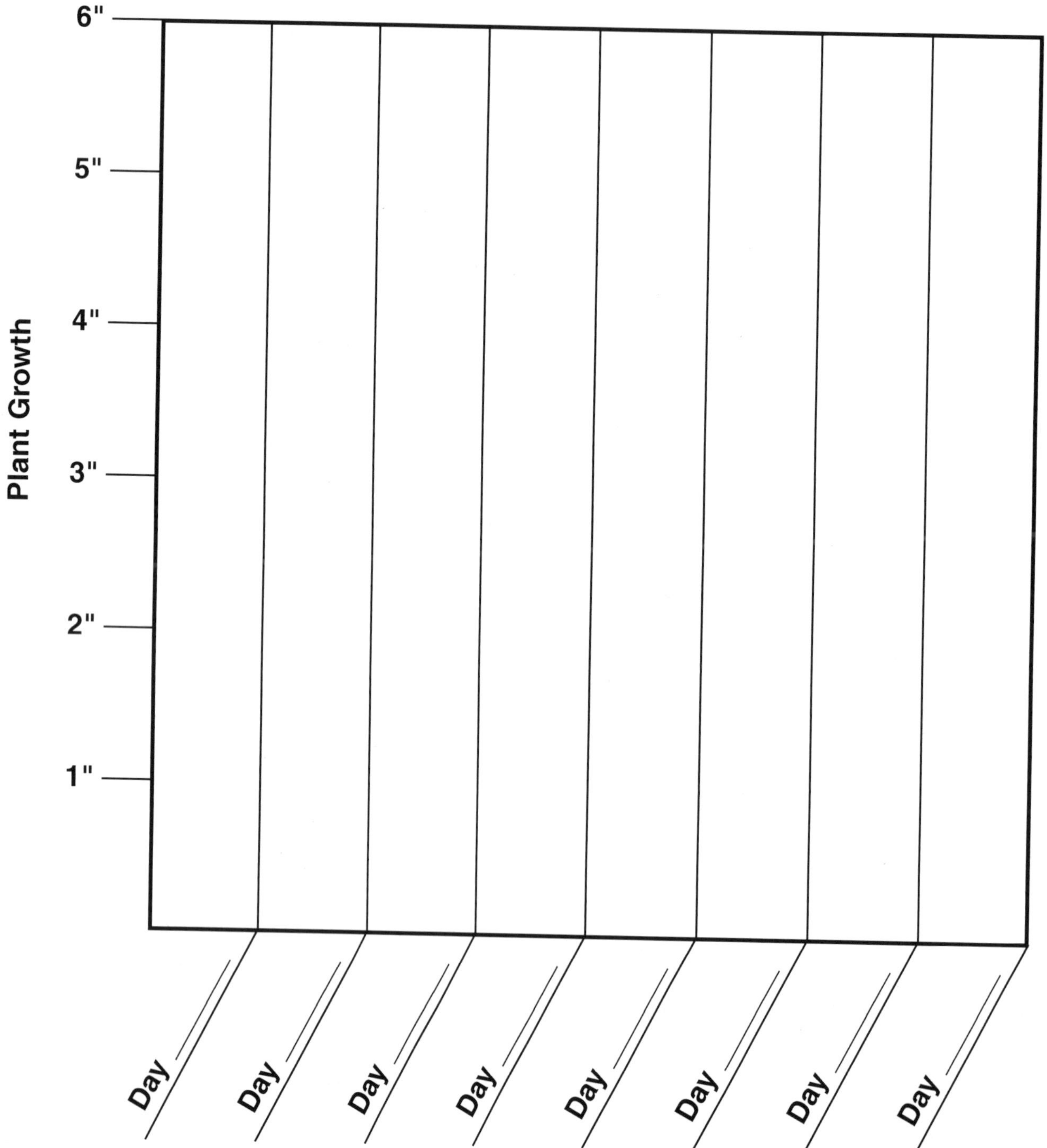

Plant Growth

6"
5"
4"
3"
2"
1"

Day ___ Day ___ Day ___ Day ___ Day ___ Day ___ Day ___ Day ___

Reading Response Journals

One great way to insure that the reading of *The Secret Garden* touches every student in a personal way is to include the use of Reading Response Journals in your plans. In these journals, students can be encouraged to respond to the story in a number of ways. Here are a few ideas.

Ask students to create a journal for *The Secret Garden*. Initially, just have them assemble lined and unlined three-holed paper in a brad-fastened report cover with a blank page for the journal's cover. As they read the story, students may draw a design on the cover that helps tell the story for them.

Tell students that the purpose of the journal is to record their thoughts, ideas, observations, and questions as they read *The Secret Garden*.

Provide students with, or ask them to suggest, topics from the story that would stimulate writing. Here are a few examples from the chapters in Section 1.

- Describe how difficult it would be to have to move to a new place where you will not know anyone at all. How might Mary feel?

- How does everyone at Misselthwaite Manor react to Mary's arrival? Do they help her to feel welcome in her new home?

- Why has Mary developed such an interest in the secret garden? Will she ever find it?

After the reading of each chapter, students can write one or more new things they learned in the chapter.

Ask student to draw their responses to certain events or characters in the story, using the blank pages in their journals.

Tell student they may use their journals to record "diary-type" responses that they may want to enter.

Encourage students to bring their journal ideas to life! Ideas generated from their journal writing can be used to create plays, debates, stories, songs, and art displays.

Allow students time to write in their journals daily. To evaluate the journals, you may wish to use the following guidelines.

Personal reflections will be read by the teacher, but no corrections or letter grades will be assigned. Credit is given for effort, and all students who sincerely try will be awarded credit. If a grade is desired for this type of entry, grade according to the number of journal entries for the number of journal assignments. For example, if five journal assignments were made and the student conscientiously completes all five, then he or she should receive an "A."

Nonjudgmental teacher responses should be made as you read the journals to let the students know that you are reading and enjoying their journals. Here are some types of responses that will please your journal writers and encourage them to write more.

"You have really found what's important in the story!"

"You write so clearly, I almost feel as if I am there!"

"If you feel comfortable doing so, I'd like you to share your ideas with the class. They will enjoy what you've written!"

Quiz Time!

1. On the back of this paper, write a one paragraph summary of the major events that happen in each of the chapters in this section. Then complete the rest of the questions on this page.

2. Describe how Mary's attitude toward Martha has changed. _____

    _____

3. How is Mary going to obtain seeds to plant in the garden? _____

    _____

4. How is Martha's mother different from Mary's mother? _____

    _____

5. Whose personal gardener had Ben Weatherstaff been?_____

    _____

6. Do you think Dickon will keep Mary's secret about the garden? Why or why not? _____

    _____

7. Why do birds like to nest in the secret garden? _____

    _____

8. Why does Mary want to plant silver bells?_____

    _____

9. Who are the "five people" that Mary likes? _____

    _____

10. Explain what "wick" means. _____

    _____

Flowers Are a Bloomin'

There are many different types of plants and flowers mentioned in *The Secret Garden*. Many of the names are probably new to you. Look at the list of flowers below. Choose several names that interest you and conduct some research about them. What type of climate do they grow in? How much sun do they need? How much water do they need? What time of year do they bloom? Do they have any smell? Report your findings to the class. Draw a sketch of the flowers you chose to research below.

heather

broom

campanulas

snowdrops

mignonette

lillies of the valley

crocuses

gorse

silverbells

roses

poppies

marigolds

canterburybells

narcissus

Personality Profiles

Many characters have been introduced in the first eight chapters of *The Secret Garden*. It is important to truly understand these people before continuing with the story. In a small group, analyze the characters by using the questions below to help generate insights into their personalities.

Mary: Describe Mary's personality. What words does the author use to describe Mary? How has Mary's personality changed since the beginning of the book? Can you think of a character from another book, T.V. show, or movie that is similar to Mary? How are they alike?

_____

_____

Mrs. Medlock: Does Mrs. Medlock have any family or children of her own? The author describes Mrs. Medlock as a woman that would "stand for no nonsense from young ones." What do you think this means? Do you think Mrs. Medlock is happy to have Mary at Misselthwaite Manor?

_____

_____

Martha: What type of person is Martha? What did she think of Mary when she first met her? Does she like her job? What does she do on her only day off each month? Does she come from a large family? What do you think Martha thinks about Mrs. Medlock?

_____

_____

Mr. Craven: Mr. Craven is an extremely wealthy man. How do you think he became so wealthy? Is he very happy? Why doesn't he want to see Mary? What might happen if they met? Does he have any family? Why do you think he travels so frequently?

_____

_____

Who are the following characters? What are they like?

Ben Weatherstaff: _____

Pitcher: _____

Dickon: _____

Magical Robin Redbreast

The robin plays a very important role in *The Secret Garden.* If it weren't for the magic of the robin, Mary may never have found the key to the secret garden.

The American robin is one of the most popular songbirds in the eastern United States. However, its name was derived from another bird, the smaller European robin. Since *The Secret Garden* takes place in Yorkshire, England, Mary's friend must be a European robin.

Do some research to find out about American robins and European robins. To help guide your research, you may try finding answers to the questions in the chart below. After you have completed the chart, answer the questions that follow.

	American Robin	European Robin
How big is the bird?		
What does it look like?		
Describe its nest.		
What do the eggs look like?		
What does it eat?		
Describe the bird's song		

How are the American robin and the European robin alike? _____

_____

How are the American robin and the European robin different? _____

_____

Challenge: It is bad luck to _____ a robin.

Home Life

Mary and Martha have very different home lives. Think about Mary's home life before she moved to Misselthwaite Manor. You may choose to reread chapters 1 and 2 to refresh your memory. Next, think about what you've read regarding Martha's home life. How are they different? Complete the chart below. Answer the questions that follow on the back of this paper.

	Mary	**Martha**
Relationships with parents		
Relationships with siblings		
Financial Means		
Responsibility at home		
Attitude toward self and others		
Education		

How have Mary and Martha's home lives shaped their personalities?

What if Martha had grown up in Mary's house and Mary had grown up in Martha's house? Would they still have the same personalities?

Think about your home life. How has it shaped your personality?

Quiz Time!

1. On the back of this paper, write a one paragraph summary of the major events that happen in each chapter in this section. Then complete the rest of the questions on this page.

2. What does Mary ask Mr. Craven for? _____

_____

3. What does Mr. Craven look like? Use details. _____

_____

4. Who is Colin? Why is he locked up in a bedroom? _____

_____

5. Why doesn't Dr. Craven want Colin to get better? _____

_____

6. Why isn't Mary afraid of Colin like everyone else is? _____

_____

7. Why is Colin crying so hysterically? _____

_____

8. What does Mary do to help Colin fall asleep? _____

_____

9. What is the good news that Mary tells Colin? _____

_____

10. Describe similarities between Colin's and Mary's personalities at the beginning of the book. Use the back of this paper if necessary.

The Secret Garden

Letter Writing

In Chapter 12, Mary is granted permission by Mr. Craven to "have a bit of earth." She is so grateful for this gift. However, because Mr. Craven is not a sociable man, after giving Mary his permission he quickly dismisses her before she can express her gratitude.

Pretend that you are Mary. Write a letter to Mr. Craven thanking him for giving you permission to plant wherever and whatever you should like. Be sure to use the proper letter writing format below, or use the format that your teacher has given you.

_____

Date

Dear Mr. Craven,
   (skip line)

   (indent) Body of letter

(indent the beginning of each paragraph)

(skip a line before closing)

Sincerely,

_____

(your name)

22

Yorkshire Speech

The Secret Garden is full of examples of the way people in Yorkshire speak. Sometimes it is easy to determine what Martha is saying and other times it is somewhat difficult. Below are several Yorkshire phrases found in *The Secret Garden*. It is your group's job to be language detectives and try to discover what these sayings mean. The first one is done for you.

1. " 'out o' doors' " __**outside; outdoors**__

2. " 'Tha'rt like th' robin' " _____

3: " 'I think tha' art th' queerest little lass I ever saw.' " _____

4. " 'Run on an' get thy victuals.' " _____

5. " 'Tha' looks as if tha'd somethin' to say.' " _____

_____

6. " 'Tha'rt not nigh so yeller and tha'rt not nigh so scrawny.' " _____

_____

7. " 'Tha' munnot waste no time.' " _____

8. " 'We mun get him watchin' an' listenin' an' sniffin' up th' air an' get him just soaked through wi' sunshine.' " _____

_____

9. " 'Tha' shouldn't have done it—tha' shouldn't! Tha'll get me in trouble.' " _____

_____

10. " 'Th' world's all fair begun again this mornin', it has. An' it's workin' an' hummin' an' scratchin' an' pipin' an nest-buildin' an' breathin' out scents, till you've got to be out on it 'stead o' lyin' on your back.' " _____

_____

Rope Skipping

Mrs. Sowerby knows that it is important for Mary to get some exercise in order to improve her health. With the little money she has, she purchases a jump rope for Mary. Mary uses the jump rope everyday while she is outside. She skips around all the gardens for many hours. As a result Mary is getting stronger and healthier.

Obtain a jump rope and try some of the following exercises.

On your own:

- jump forward

- jump backward

- hop on one foot forward

- hop on one foot backward

- jump "jumping jack" style (legs apart, then together)

- jump forward criss-crossing arms

- jump while skipping

With four or more people:

Have two people hold the rope while two others try the following:

- jump while holding hands

- do a half turn each time you jump

In a large group:

Have two people hold the jump rope. Next, see how many people can:

- jump together at the same time

- jump in all at once and then out together

- jump in at the same time

- turn around together

- recite jump rope rhymes

- call out birthday months and then jump in when called

It's a challenge!

Rainy Day Fun

Shortly after Mary and Dickon begin working on the secret garden they run into some very bad weather. It rains in Yorkshire for almost an entire week! Because of the bad weather, Mary is forced to amuse herself inside the house. She decides to wander around the many rooms in Misselthwaite Manor that she has been curious about since she arrived.

Name five other activities Mary could do on rainy days.

1. _____
2. _____
3. _____
4 _____
5. _____

Suppose that Mary and Colin had already been friends before the bad weather started. What activities could they do together on rainy days?

1. _____
2. _____
3. _____
4. _____
5. _____

Describe some activities that you do when you can't go outside to play.

1. _____
2. _____
3. _____

With a partner, make up a game that you can play on a rainy day. Write the directions. Exchange with another group and try playing each other's games.

Quiz Time!

1. On the back of this paper, write a one paragraph summary of the major events that happen in each of the chapters of this section. Then complete the rest of the questions on this page.

2. What does Mrs. Sowerby mean when she says, "There's no sense in grabbin' at th' whole orange?"

   _____

   _____

3. Why does Colin suddenly believe that he will live forever?

   _____

   _____

4. Why does Dickon become nervous when Colin asks about the broken branch in the garden?

   _____

   _____

5. How does Ben Weatherstaff react when he sees Mary, Dickon, and Colin in the garden?

   _____

   _____

6. Explain the experiment that Colin is going to conduct.

   _____

   _____

7. What is the new secret that the children have?

   _____

   _____

8. What does Colin want to be when he grows up?

   _____

   _____

9. Why do Colin and Mary think that there is magic in the garden?

   _____

   _____

10. Have you ever had a special moment when you felt as though you would live forever? Describe it.

    _____

    _____

Advice Column

Dr. Craven has been told not to contact Archibald Craven regarding Colin's health. The dilemma for Dr. Craven lies in the fact that he is Colin's doctor and he has an obligation to report to Mr. Craven. Dr. Craven is caught in the middle between Colin's demands and his duty to Archibald Craven. What should he do?

Pretend you are an advice columnist and on a separate piece of paper, answer the letter from Dr. Craven below.

Dear Friend,

      I am a medical doctor. I have many patients, ranging in age from newborn to over 60. The children that I care for always visit along with their parents. I am careful to make sure that the parents know and understand everything about their child's health. Because of my forthrightness, I have never had any problems with patients or parents...until now. My cousin, Archibald Craven, has a son who is very ill. Along with the many viruses he has, he is also a hunchback. We do not expect him to live very long. In the past, I have kept my cousin up to date on Colin's prognosis. Usually, there is little to report because his condition remains dreadful. However, recently there have been some changes. Colin appears to be growing stronger and his appetite has increased. Even his personality has changed for the better! I was quite anxious to report this news to my cousin, but Colin has forbidden me to do any such thing. I feel that I have an obligation to tell my cousin, yet, I do not want to deal with one of Colin's tantrums if he finds out that I have contacted his father. What should I do?

Signed,

Baffled Doctor

Visit a Nursery

In this activity, you will need to visit a nursery in order to receive some general information to be used in a later assignment. Follow the instructions below and then answer the questions.

Preparing for your visit

- Locate a yellow pages.

- Find several local nurseries that you and a friend could visit.

- Phone these nurseries and ask what their business hours are.

- Based on the information gathered, choose the nursery that you will visit.

- Arrange for you and a friend to get to the nursery.

- Prepare questions that you may have about plants and gardens so that you can ask the attendant at the nursery.

1. _____

2. _____

3. _____

While at the nursery:

- Ask to see some of the flowers mentioned in *The Secret Garden* or some that you have researched. Make a sketch of what you saw.

- Ask how you would go about choosing flowers for a garden. Take notes on this information for use in a later assignment.

- Choose several flowers that you would like to plant if you had your own garden. List them below along with their price. This information will be useful to you in a later assignment.

Fun With Food

In hotels and in homes, more and more people are meeting in the middle to late afternoon to observe a charming old English custom, formal tea. It is a time to bring out your tea service and enjoy socializing with close friends.

Use the recipes below to help you prepare a formal tea service. Perhaps you can invite parents or another class to attend. In any case, you are sure to enjoy this English tradition.

Tea

1. Bring freshly drawn water to a full boil.
2. Use one teaspoonful (5 mL) or 1 bag of tea for each cup of water.
3. Let the tea brew 3-5 minutes. Some teas brew light and some dark. With this in mind, be sure to brew by time, not color.
4. Stir tea before pouring it. Serve with lemon or milk.

Ginger Tea Cake

Ingredients: 2 cups (500 mL) unsifted all-purpose flour, 1 teaspoon (5 mL) baking powder, 1 cup (250 mL) butter or margarine, 1 cup (250 mL) granulated sugar, 4 eggs, ½ cup (125 mL) chopped preserved ginger in syrup, 2 tablespoons (30 mL) syrup from preserved ginger.

1. Sift flour with baking powder and set aside.
2. Preheat oven to 300°F (150°C). Grease and flour an 8½ (22 cm) by 4½ (11 cm) by 2½" (6 cm) loaf pan.
3. In a large bowl, at medium speed, cream butter with granulated sugar until very light and fluffy. Gradually beat in eggs, one at a time, beating well after each addition. Beat in ½ cup (125 mL) ginger and the ginger syrup.
4. At low speed, stir in flour mixture until combined. Do not over beat.
5. Pour into prepared pan. Bake 1¾ hours or until cake tester comes out clean. Cover top loosely with foil during last 15 minutes to prevent over browning.
6. Let cool on wire rack 10-15 minutes. Remove cake from pan and cool completely.

English Raisin Cookies

Ingredients: 3½ cups (875 mL) sifted all-purpose flour, ½ teaspoon (2.5 mL) baking soda, ½ teaspoon (2.5 mL) salt, 1 teaspoon (5 mL) ground cinnamon, 1 teaspoon (5 mL) ground nutmeg, ½ cup (125 mL) butter or margarine, softened, 1 cup (250 mL) sugar, 2 eggs, ½ cup (125 mL) sour cream, cup (250 mL) finely chopped raisins.

1. Sift flour with baking soda, salt, cinnamon, and nutmeg. Set aside.
2. In large bowl, with wooden spoon, beat butter, sugar, and eggs until light and fluffy.
3. Add sour cream, raisins, and flour mixture; mix thoroughly.
4. With rubber scraper, form dough into ball. Wrap with wax paper and refrigerate 1 hour.
5. Divide dough into four parts; refrigerate until ready to roll.
6. Preheat oven to 375°F (190°C). Lightly grease cookie sheets.
7. On lightly floured surface, roll dough into a 12" X 14" (30 cm X 36 cm) rectangle. With sharp floured knife cut dough diagonally to make diamond shapes.
8. Using spatula, place 1½" (4 cm) apart on cookie sheets. Bake 8-10 minutes. Makes 6 dozen.

Getting to Know You

You must be quite familiar with all the characters in *The Secret Garden* by now. Each of the main characters in the story are listed below:

Mary	**Martha**	**Mr. Craven**
Colin	**Ben**	**Dr. Craven**
Dickon	**Mrs. Sowerby**	**Mrs. Medlock**

Choose one of the characters above that you would most like to spend an entire day with. Then, answer the questions below.

1. Which character did you choose?

2. Why did you choose that character?

3. What do you and that character have in common?

4. List at least three questions that you will ask that character when you meet him or her.

    1.

    2.

    3.

5. On the back of this paper, describe in detail what you will do on the one day that you have together.

Quiz Time!

1. On the back of this paper, write a one paragraph summary of the major events in each chapter of this section. Then complete the rest of the questions on this page.

2. Why is Colin so angry that Dr. Craven wanted to write to his father?

   _____

   _____

3. What does the robin compare Colin's walking to?

   _____

   _____

4. Explain what Mary and Colin do on rainy days.

   _____

   _____

5. Why does Ben Weatherstaff cry after they sing the prayer?

   _____

   _____

6. What is Colin's wish regarding Mrs. Sowerby?

   _____

   _____

7. What makes Mrs. Sowerby decide to write to Mr. Craven? What does she say to him?

   _____

   _____

8. What is Colin doing to help his muscles get stronger?

   _____

   _____

9. How do Colin and his father reunite? How did you feel at this moment?

   _____

   _____

10. Write a poem about the secret garden. It can be any kind of poem that you choose. Here are just a few ideas: acrostic, diamante, haiku, and rhyme.

The New Garden

Mary, Dickon, and Colin have put countless hours into beautifying the secret garden. Draw a picture of what you think the garden may look like now. When you have finished drawing your picture, compare it to the one you drew at the beginning of the book. What are the differences? Is anything the same? You may wish to mount both pictures on a large piece of construction paper for comparison.

Look to the Future

When the book ends, Mary, Colin, and Dickon are still very young. Frances Hodgson Burnett hinted about what the future may have in store for these children, but nothing was stated directly. This is your opportunity to predict what may happen to Mary, Colin, and Dickon in the future. It might also be fun to predict the future of Martha, Mr. Craven, and Ben Weatherstaff. Use the ideas below to help make your predictions. This may be your only chance to be a fortune teller!

Prediction Ideas:

occupation	marriage
children	financial means
hobbies	pets
friends	city or town living in

My prediction for Mary is:

My prediction for Colin is:

My Prediction for Dickon is:

My prediction for Martha is:

My prediction for Mr. Craven is:

My prediction for Ben Weatherstaff is:

Crossword Puzzle

Across

2. resisting control
4. dramatic disclosure of something not already known
6. a turbulent swift flowing stream
7. a person who withdraws from the world
10. a narrow hallway
14. go smoothly through the air
16. puzzled or confused
17. constantly ill
18. a person who thinks they are ill, but they are not
19. a long extension of a stem

Down

1. request information
3. stubbornly adhering to an attitude or opinion
5. showing odd behavior
6. a fit of bad temper
8. nonsensical rapid talk
9. relating to disease
10. angry
11. showing determination
12. uncontrollable crying
13. a digging tool
15. a broad piece of open land

Word List

corridor	invalid	recluse	cross	moor
revelation	determined	morbid	spade	gibberish
obstinate	tantrum	hypochondriac	perplexed	tendril
hysterics	queer	torrent	inquire	rebellious
		waft		

Your Own Secret Place

Mary, Colin, and Dickon all loved the peace and solitude of having their own secret place. The garden provided a safe, secret place for them to go to be together. They loved their secret place so much that they did not mind the hours on top of hours they had to spend to make it beautiful. This is sometimes referred to as a "labor of love." They loved the garden and therefore the planting work became fun. There are probably times when we all wish for a secret place to go. Using the questions below as a guide, you will create your own secret place.

Where is your secret place? *(Be specific.)*

Why would you go to your secret place? *(Be specific.)*

When would you go to your secret place? *(Be specific.)*

What would you do in your secret place? *(Be specific.)*

Would you tell anyone about your secret place? *(Who would you tell?)*

What does your secret place look like? You may wish to draw a picture of it.

Any Questions?

When you finished reading *The Secret Garden*, did you have any questions that were left unanswered? Write some of your questions here.

_____

_____

_____

Work in groups or by yourself to prepare possible answers for some or all of the questions you have asked above and those written below. When you have finished your predictions, share your ideas with the class.

- Will Mary, Colin, and Dickon continue to care for the secret garden?

- Will Mary begin school with a governess?

- Will Mr. Craven continue to travel now that Colin is well?

- Now that Colin is better, will Dr. Craven continue to care for him?

- Does the garden continue to grow as well as it has?

- Do the robin and his family continue to live in the secret garden?

- Will Dickon remain friends with Mary and Colin?

- Does Colin ever develop a hunchback?

- Do Colin and his father become closer now that Colin is better?

- Does Mary ever move away from Misselthwaite Manor?

- What will become of Mrs. Medlock?

- Will Mr. Craven finally talk more freely about Mrs. Craven to Colin?

- Does Mary still need Martha to look after her? If not, what happens to Martha?

- Does Ben become the gardener for the secret garden?

- How will Misselthwaite Manor change now that Colin is well?

Book Report Ideas

There are numerous ways to report on a book once you have read it. After you finish reading *The Secret Garden,* choose one method of reporting on the book that interests you. It may be a way that your teacher suggests, an idea of your own, or one of the ways that is mentioned below.

- **See What I Read?**

  This report is a visual one. A model of a scene from the story can be created, or a likeness of one or more of the characters from the story can be drawn or sculpted.

- **Come To Life!**

  This report is one that lends itself to a group project. A size-appropriate group prepares a scene from the story for dramatization, acts it out, and relates the significance of the scene to the entire book. Costumes and props will add to the dramatization.

- **Into the Future**

  This report predicts what might happen if *The Secret Garden* were to continue. It may take the form of a story in narrative of dramatic form, or a visual display.

- **A Letter to a Character**

  In this report, you may write a letter to any character in the story. You may ask him or her any questions that you wish. You may even want to offer some advice on a particular problem.

- **Guess Who or What!**

  This report is similar to "Twenty Questions." The reporter gives a series of clues about a character or event in the story in a vague or precise, general to specific order. After all clues have been given, the character or event must be deduced.

- **Mary Returns!**

  Write a whole new story using Mary as the main character. Other characters from *The Secret Garden* may also be used.

- **Star Reporter!**

  Write an event the same way a reporter would. Choose a headline that will draw attention to the story. You may include quotes that you think would be appropriate for the character to say.

Research Ideas

Describe three things you read in *The Secret Garden* that you would like to learn more about.

1. _____

2. _____

3. _____

As you are reading *The Secret Garden,* you will encounter geographical locations, historical events, diverse people, ways of life that are different from your own, and a variety of animals and plants. To increase your understanding of the characters and events in the story as well as more fully realize Frances Hodgson Burnett's craft as a writer, research to find out more about these people, places, habits, and things.

Work in groups to research one or more of the areas you named above, or the areas that are mentioned below. Share your findings with the rest of the class in any appropriate form of oral presentation.

- Yorkshire, England
  - customs
  - food
  - economy
  - history
  - physical features
  - weather
- India
  - customs
  - food
  - colonization
- cholera
  - symptoms
  - transmission
  - treatment

- gardening
  - tools
  - plants
  - vegetables
- animals
  - squirrel
  - fox
  - robin
  - crow
- hunchbacks
- nursery rhymes
- moors
  - locations
  - weather conditions

Design Your Own Garden

Teacher Note: Your students will be designing their own garden. Using what they have learned about plants from reading *The Secret Garden* and doing their own research, students will select plants and design a secret garden all their own.

Mary, Colin, and Dickon have had the time of their lives creating their own secret garden. In this unit, you have conducted research on different types of plants and even done some planting of your own. For this activity, you will create your own secret garden. Where it is located and what is planted is totally up to YOU! Use the following questions to help guide you in making decisions about your garden.

Where will your secret garden be?

What type of climate is it?

How much space do you have?

How often will you be available to care for the garden?

What colors do you like?

Do you or does anyone who will be in the garden frequently have any allergies?

Design Your Own Garden

Based on the requirements and preferences you outlined in the previous assignment, you must now choose what to plant in your garden. You may wish to use your notes from your visit to the nursery. Or perhaps a second trip is required to obtain more information. Use the guide below to help you with your decision making. Make notes about what you wish to buy.

	What I would like to buy	Cost	Check (✔) items purchased
Ground Cover			
Trees			
Flowers			
Bushes			
Total			

Design Your Own Garden

Draw a detailed plan of your secret garden. Show where each of the plants that you have chosen will be planted. Use crayons or markers to make the pictures as colorful as possible.

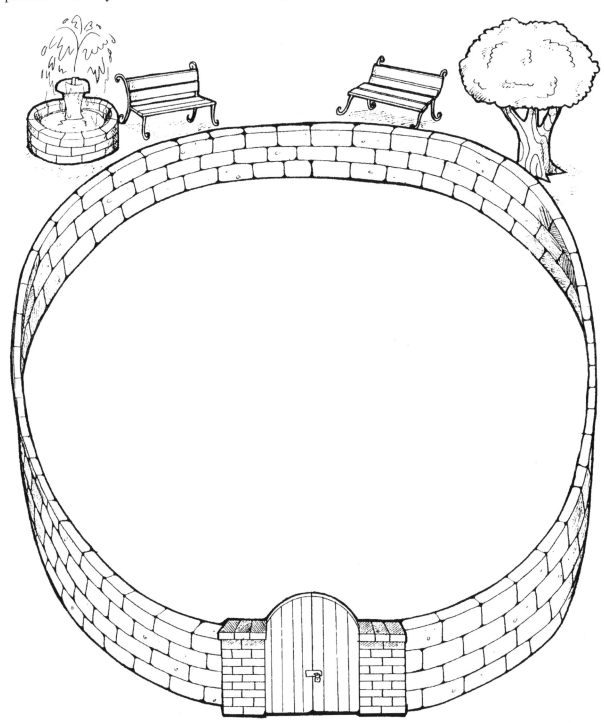

Now that you have planned and designed your own garden, imagine what it would be like to be inside of it. Write a story about a day that you spent in your secret garden. Be as descriptive as Frances Hodgson Burnett was when she described Mary, Colin and Dickon's experiences in their garden.

Unit Test

Matching: Match the vocabulary word with its synonym.

1. _____	obstinate	A. emptiness
2. _____	queer	B. wise
3. _____	desolation	C. stubborn
4. _____	condescend	D. conceited
5. _____	shrewd	E. ruthless
6. _____	astonished	F. surprised
7 _____	vain	G. talk down to
8. _____	unscrupulous	H. strange

True or False: Write true or false next to each statement below.

1. _____ Mary's parents died of cholera.

2. _____ Martha receives one day off per month.

3. _____ Ben Weatherstaff never met Mrs. Craven.

4. _____ Mrs. Craven died after falling from a tree branch.

5. _____ Mr. Craven never leaves his house because he is embarrassed about his hunchback.

Short Answer: Provide a short answer for each question.

1. Why did Mary want to find the secret garden? _____

2. Who helped Mary find the key to the secret garden? _____

3. Why did Colin suddenly decide he wanted to go outside? _____

4. Where did Mary get the seeds to plant in the garden? _____

5. Why wouldn't Dr. Craven want Colin to get better?_____

Essay: Answer these questions on the back of this paper.

1. Why do you suppose that two disagreeable children like Mary and Colin get along so well?

2. Explain why Mr. Craven cut his trip short and decided to return home.

Response

Explain the meaning of each of these quotations from *The Secret Garden*.

Chapter 2:   " 'My word! She's a plain little piece of goods! And we'd heard that her mother was a beauty. She hasn't handed much of it down, has she, ma'am?' "

Chapter 4:   " 'People never like me and I never like people.' "

Chapter 7:   " 'Tha' young vixen, tha'! There tha' stands sayin' tha' doesn't like this one an' tha' doesn't like that one. How does tha' like thysel'?' "

Chapter 9:   " 'No wonder it is still. I am the first person who has spoken in here for ten years.' "

Chapter 10:   " 'It's a secret garden, and I'm the only one in the world who wants it to be   alive.' "

Chapter 12:   " 'You remind me of someone else who loved the earth and things that grow. When you see a bit of earth you want, take it child, and make it come alive.' "

Chapter 13:   " 'The rain is as contrary as I ever was.' "

Chapter 15:   " 'Ben Weatherstaff says that he is so conceited he would rather have stones thrown at him than not be noticed.' "

Chapter 16:   " 'If he'd had a young vixen of a sister to fight with, it would have been the saving of him.' "

Chapter 20:   " 'Let's hope they're changing for the better, Mrs. Medlock. They couldn't well change for the worse.' "

Chapter 21:   " 'It was Magic which sent the robin.' "

Chapter 22:   " 'Tha die! Nowt o' th' sort! Tha's got too much pluck in thee.' "

Chapter 25:   " 'Now that I am a real boy my legs and arms and all my body are so full of Magic that I can't keep them still.' "

Chapter 27:   " 'To tell the truth, sir, Master Colin might be better and he might be changing for the worse.' "

Teacher Note: Choose an appropriate number of quotes for your students.

Conversations

Work in size-appropriate groups to write and perform the conversations that might have occurred in each of the following situations.

- Dr. Craven calls Mr. Craven to tell him what's going on at Misselthwaite Manor with regard to Colin's sudden improving health. (2 people)

- Mr. Craven tells Mrs. Medlock that Mary will be coming to live with them because her parents have passed away. (2 people)

- Mrs. Medlock informs Martha that she will have to care for Mary. (2 people)

- Martha tells her mother and family about how Mary can't do anything for herself. (5+people)

- Ben Weatherstaff tells Mrs. Medlock that he saw Mary playing in the garden. (2 people)

- Dickon and Mrs. Sowerby discuss Mary's desire to plant seeds. (2 people)

- Mrs. Medlock explains to the servants that Mary is a disagreeable child used to having her own way. (3 people)

- The servants discuss the shouting match between Mary and Colin the night before. (3 or more people)

- Mary, Colin, and Dickon explain to Mr. Craven how they found the garden and why they decided to begin taking care of it. (4 people)

- Ben Weatherstaff and Mr. Craven reminisce about how Mrs. Craven loved the garden. (2 people)

- Mr. Craven expresses his displeasure to Dr. Craven for not contacting him about what was happening with Colin. (2 people)

- Mary, Colin, and Dickon make plans to continue working in the garden. (3 people)

- Mr. Craven thanks Mrs. Sowerby for writing the letter to him. (2 people)

Write and perform one of your own conversation ideas for the characters from *The Secret Garden.*

Bibliography

Babbitt, Natalie. *Tuck Everlasting.* (Farrar, Straus, & Giroux, 1875)

Burnett, Frances Hodgson. *Little Lord Fauntleroy.* (Scribner, 1886)

Burnett, Frances Hodgson. *A Little Princess.* (Scribner, 1905)

Burnett, Frances Hodgson. *The Lost Prince.* (Century, 1915)

Burnett, Frances Hodgson. *Sara Crewe.* (Scribuer, 1888)

Cleary, Beverly. *The Mouse and the Motorcycle.* (Dell Publishing, 1965)

Cleary, Beverly. *Ralph S. Mouse.* (Dell Publishing, 1982)

Gardiner, John Reynolds. *Stone Fox.* (Thomas Y. Crowell, 1980)

Grahame, Kenneth. *The Wind in the Willows.* (Scribner, 1908)

Hutchins, Ross E. *The Amazing Seeds.* (Dodd, Mead, 1965)

Kipling, Rudyard. *Just So Stories.* (Doubleday, 1902)

Konigsburg, E.L. *From the Mixed-Up Files of Mrs. Basil E. Frankweiler.* (Atheneum, 1967)

Lawson, Robert. *Rabbit Hill.* (Puffin Books, 1944)

L'Engle, Madeleine. *Dragons in the Waters.* (Dell Publishing, 1976)

Lewis, C.S. *The Lion, the Witch and the Wardrobe.* (Macmillan Publishing Company, 1950)

Lofting, Hugh. *The Story of Doctor Dolittle.* (Lippincott-Stokes, 1920)

MacLachlan, Patricia. *The Facts and Fictions of Minna Pratt.* (Harper and Row, 1988)

Paterson, Katherine. *Bridge to Terabithia.* (Crowell, 1977)

Paterson, Katherine. *The Great Gilly Hopkins.* (Harper and Row, 1978)

Pearce, Philippa A. *Tom's Midnight Garden.* University Press, 1958)

Rawls, Wilson. *Where the Red Fern Grows.* (Bantam, 1985)

Answer Key

Page 10

1. Accept appropriate responses.
2. Mary has to live with her uncle because her parents have died.
3. Mary thinks Misselthwaite Manor looks cold, dark, and scary.
4. Martha thinks Mary is a spoiled child who can do nothing for herself.
5. Dickon is Martha's brother. He is very nice and down to earth.
6. Mr. Craven locked the garden after his wife died inside.
7. Mary explored the house when it was raining.
8. Mrs. Medlock was furious to find Mary wandering around.
9. Mary wants to visit Martha's house.
10. Accept appropriate drawings.

Page 16

1. Accept appropriate responses.
2. Mary no longer regards Martha as a servant. Martha is now a friend.
3. Mary has asked Dickon to purchase seeds and bring them to her.
4. Martha's mother is very active in the lives of her children. Mary's mother was not.
5. Ben Weatherstaff was Mrs. Craven's gardener.
6. Accept appropriate responses.
7. Birds nest in the garden because it is quiet and peaceful.
8. Mary wants to plant silver bells because they remind her of the rhyme that the children at the clergyman's house sang to her.
9. Mary likes Dickon, Mrs. Sowerby, Martha, Ben, and the robin.
10. Wick means alive.

Page 19

Answers may vary. You may wish to have students cite sources.

Challenge: It is bad luck to kill a robin.

Page 21

1. Accept appropriate responses.
2. A bit of earth.
3. Mr. Craven has high, crooked shoulders, a hunchback, and black hair streaked with white.
4. Colin is Mr. Craven's son. He is kept in his bedroom because he is very sick.
5. Dr. Craven will inherit Misselthwaite Manor if Colin dies.
6. Mary is just as stubborn and disagreeable as Colin and therefore he does not scare her.
7. Colin cried because he thought he felt a lump on his back.
8. Mary sings to Colin to help him fall asleep.
9. Mary told Colin that she had found the secret garden.
10. Colin and Mary are both spoiled and stubborn. They are both disagreeable to servants. They care only for themselves.

Answer Key *(cont.)*

Page 23

These are suggested answers. Accept all reasonable responses.

1. outside
2. You are like the robin.
3. I think you are the strangest girl I have ever seen.
4. Run along and get your dinner.
5. You look as if you have something to say.
6. You are no longer so yellow or so scrawny.
7. You musn't waste any time.
8. We must get him to watch and listen and smell the air and become soaked through with sunshine.
9. You shouldn't have done it—you shouldn't have. You will get me in trouble.
10. The world is starting over this morning. And it's working and humming and scratching and breaking out and building nests and giving out scents until you just have to be outside instead of inside lying around.

Page 26

1. Accept appropriate responses.
2. Mrs. Sowerby meant that children shouldn't try to get more than their fair share or they may end up with nothing.
3. Colin felt so good outside that he felt he might get stronger and live forever.
4. Dickon was afraid to tell Colin that his mother had died from a branch that broke in the garden.
5. Ben was angry when he saw the children in the garden.
6. Colin was trying to find out if he could get better by exercising.
7. The children have made the garden beautiful once again.
8. Colin wants to be a scientist when he grows up.
9. Colin and Mary think there must be magic in the garden because Colin has gotten well and they have been able to make the garden beautiful again.
10. Accept appropriate responses.

Page 31

1. Accept appropriate responses.
2. Colin wants to surprise his father when he returns home.
3. The robin thought that Colin looked like a baby bird trying to walk.
4. Mary and Colin explore the mansion on rainy days.
5. Ben cried because he thought of Mrs. Craven. Also because the garden was like a miracle.
6. Colin wishes Mrs. Sowerby could be his mother.
7. Mrs. Sowerby thought Mr. Craven would be happy if he knew what the children did in the garden.
8. Colin is doing exercises to get stronger.
9. Colin ran into his father after a race with Mary.

Answer Key *(cont.)*

Page 34

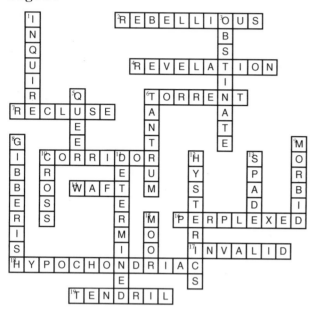

Page 42

1. C 2. H 3. A. 4. G. 5. B. 6. F 7. D 8. E

1. True 2. True 3. False 4. True 5. False

1. Mary was intrigued by the garden.

2. The robin helped Mary.

3. Colin wants to see the secret garden.

4. Dickon gave Mary the seeds.

5. Dr. Craven wants to inherit the mansion.

For Essay questions, accept appropriate responses.

Page 43

Accept appropriate responses.

Page 44

Perform the conversation in class. Ask students to respond in ways such as, "Are the conversations realistic?" or "Are the words the character say typical of their personalities?"

Made in the USA
Middletown, DE
06 February 2018